MICHAEL

LIFE Books

EDITOR Robert Sullivan
DIRECTOR OF PHOTOGRAPHY Barbara Baker Burrows
CREATIVE DIRECTOR Mimi Park
DEPUTY PICTURE EDITOR Christina Lieberman
WRITER-REPORTER Hildegard Anderson
COPY EDITORS Danielle Dowling, Barbara Gogan, Parlan McGaw
CONSULTING PICTURE EDITORS Sarah Burrows, Mimi Murphy (Rome),
Tala Skari (Paris)
SPECIAL THANKS Martha Robson Bardach, Crary Pullen

PRESIDENT Andrew Blau
BUSINESS MANAGER Roger Adler
BUSINESS DEVELOPMENT MANAGER Jeff Burak

TIME INC. HOME ENTERTAINMENT
PUBLISHER Richard Fraiman
GENERAL MANAGER Steven Sandonato
EXECUTIVE DIRECTOR, MARKETING SERVICES Carol Pittard
DIRECTOR, RETAIL & SPECIAL SALES Tom Mifsud
DIRECTOR, NEW PRODUCT DEVELOPMENT Peter Harper
ASSISTANT DIRECTOR, BOOKAZINE MARKETING Laura Adam
ASSISTANT PUBLISHING DIRECTOR, BRAND MARKETING Joy Butts
ASSOCIATE COUNSEL Helen Wan
BOOK PRODUCTION MANAGER Susan Chodakiewicz
DESIGN & PREPRESS MANAGER Anne-Michelle Gallero
BRAND MANAGER Shelley Rescober

EDITORIAL OPERATIONS Richard K. Prue (Director), Brian Fellows (Manager),
Keith Aurelio, Charlotte Coco, John Goodman, Kevin Hart, Norma Jones,
Mert Kerimoglu, Rosalie Khan, Patricia Koh, Marco Lau, Brian Mai,
Po Fung Ng, Lorenzo Pace, Rudi Papiri, Robert Pizaro, Barry Pribula,
Clara Renauro, Donald Schaedtler, Hia Tan, Vaune Trachtman, David Weiner

SPECIAL THANKS Christine Austin, Glenn Buonocore, Jim Childs,
Rose Cirrincione, Jacqueline Fitzgerald, Lauren Hall, Jennifer Jacobs,
Suzanne Janso, Brynn Joyce, Mona Li, Robert Marasco, Amy Migliaccio,
Brooke Reger, Dave Rozzelle, Ilene Schreider, Adriana Tierno,
Alex Voznesenskiy, Sydney Webber, Jonathan White

Published by LIFE Books

Time Inc.
1271 Avenue of the Americas
New York, NY 10020

ISBN 13: 978-1-60320-130-8
ISBN 10: 1-60320-130-0
Library of Congress Control Number: 2009931793

"LIFE" is a trademark of Time Inc.

We welcome your comments and suggestions about LIFE Books.
Please write to us at:
LIFE Books
Attention: Book Editors
PO Box 11016
Des Moines, IA 50336-1016

If you would like to order any of our hardcover
Collector's Edition books, please call us at 1-800-327-6388
(Monday through Friday, 7:00 a.m.–8:00 p.m.,
or Saturday, 7:00 a.m.–6:00 p.m., Central Time).

Visit Us at LIFE.com

Simply put, this site has the most amazing collection of professional
photography on the Web, with millions of iconic images
from LIFE magazine's archives, never-before-seen LIFE pictures and
up-to-the-minute news photos. Come see for yourself!

ENDPAPERS: In a photo seen here for the first time, the young teen sprints
through a park in Beverly Hills, California, in 1973. Photograph by Jim Britt.
PAGE 1: In California, in 1971.
Photograph by Henry Diltz/Morrison Hotel Gallery.
PAGES 2–3: In the movie theater of the family home in Encino, California,
in 1983. Photograph by Todd Gray.
THIS PAGE: Expressing humility during a concert at Yokahama Stadium
in Japan in 1987. Photograph by Neal Preston.

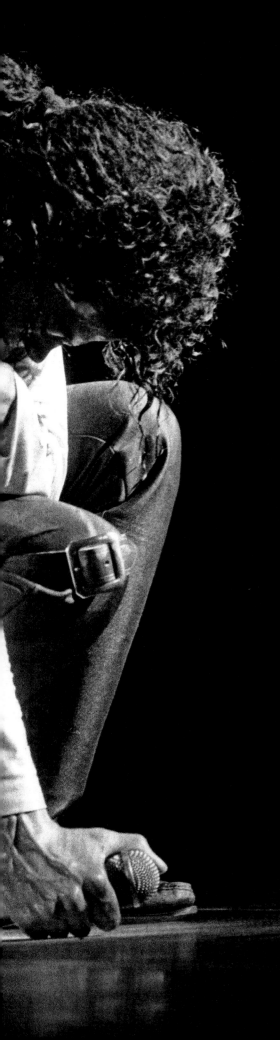

Contents

His LIFE

When you become a celebrity during your preteen years in the United States, the photographic record of your life will be deep. Indeed it is that in the case of Michael Jackson. His picture was taken early and often, and so many photographs presented to the public brought an instant smile.

The joyous boy, so obviously thrilled with his luck and success. The dancer, gliding forward and backward, an icon in aspect. The celebrity celebrated by an adoring crowd.

So many images . . .

It is a large visual record to be sure. But is it substantial? Does it capture him?

In the case of Michael Jackson, so many photographs were taken from a considerable distance, either geographically or emotionally. To use a more descriptive word, many pictures were taken at a *remove*.

Why? Well, shots of pop stars performing are what they are, with some being better than others—and we hope we have chosen the best of those for our book. Then, too, Michael Jackson led an inarguably unusual life offstage, and writers and photographers trying to feed the 24-hour news cycle understandably took what crumbs they could find. Jackson became wary of the press, perhaps because he knew that his adult story would not—could not—play well alongside the sweetness-and-light chapter that was the Jackson 5. He built his cocoon. He did not reveal himself willingly as time went on, save for a couple—and it is only a couple—of candid interviews. And a precious few photo sessions.

As might be assumed, LIFE magazine, then the country's preeminent picture magazine, was early with the story of the Jackson 5. In fact, when we sent John Olson out to shoot a now-famous photo essay on rockers and their parents—a feature that included Eric Clapton and his grandmum and Elton John with his folks—the Jacksons not only graced our pages but made the cover (and in this book, you will see an alternate frame that has never before been published—featuring little Janet!). For whatever his personal reasons, Michael trusted LIFE and opened his doors thereafter—even the doors to Neverland, which were firmly closed to others. Twice on

assignment for LIFE in the 1990s, the storied Scottish photojournalist Harry Benson—who had realized early fame with his pictures of the Beatles, including the pillow-fight shot in a Paris hotel room and the photo of them deplaning at Kennedy Airport in 1964—took exquisite, intimate portraits of Jackson. (His two LIFE covers of Jackson are seen on the bottom row, opposite; Olson's shot of the family is at the top left.) At the other end of the spectrum, when the Jacksons were at their apex during the 1984 Victory Tour, we sent Henry Groskinsky, the magazine's top technical wizard, to capture that spectacle in a way no one else could.

Those pictures are in this book, of course, but we freely admit that they would not tell the complete story. And so we have assembled the best of all the portfolios available, including those of the famous rock 'n' roll shooters Neal Preston and Lynn Goldsmith; Goldsmith shot the cover at the top right, opposite, exclusively for LIFE. Characteristically, LIFE's longtime photo-editing team of Barbara Baker Burrows and Christina Lieberman has unearthed some wondrous finds, among them several never-before-seen pictures, including an altogether engaging set by Jim Britt, who spent quality time with Michael when he was right on the cusp of graduating from the Jackson 5. That was an exciting time, and those are exciting photographs, owing in no small part to their concentrated intimacy.

There are words in this book, too, and we're pleased with them—we feel that they tell Michael Jackson's story honestly, completely and, we hope, eloquently. But we brag on our pictures. This is, we again hope, *the* illustrated biography of one of the two or three or four seminal American entertainers of the 20th century, one of the two or three who changed our culture and our society. His was an extraordinary life, and on the pages that follow, you will gaze upon some extraordinary pictures.

LIFE

ROCK STARS AT HOME WITH THEIR PARENTS

The Jackson Five
with Mom and Pop

JACKSON 5 BLVD   JACKSON 5

SEPTEMBER 24 • 1971 • 50¢

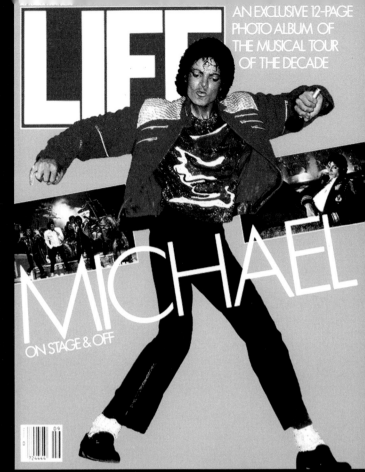

LIFE

AN EXCLUSIVE 12-PAGE PHOTO ALBUM OF THE MUSICAL TOUR OF THE DECADE

MICHAEL
ON STAGE & OFF

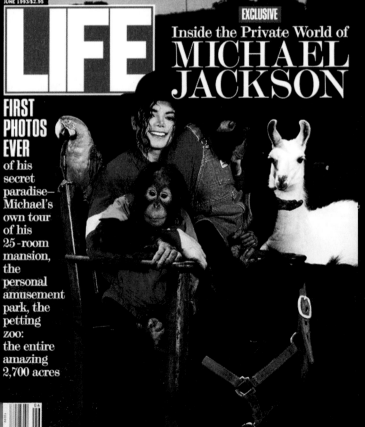

JUNE 1993/$2.95

LIFE

EXCLUSIVE
Inside the Private World of
MICHAEL JACKSON

FIRST PHOTOS EVER of his secret paradise— Michael's own tour of his 25-room mansion, the personal amusement park, the petting zoo: the entire amazing 2,700 acres

LIFE

EXCLUSIVE
Michael & Son
AT HOME WITH THE KING OF POP AND HIS BABY

HOLIDAY BONUS

WHAT IS THE SOUL?

MEDITATIONS FROM:
DEEPAK CHOPRA
SHIRLEY MacLAINE
MARIANNE WILLIAMSON
REV. GEORGE FOREMAN
AND **35** OTHERS

DECEMBER 1997/$3.95
DISPLAY UNTIL DECEMBER 22

Michael
the
Moonwalker

To be able to float free, with gravity exerting no impact.
To live in Neverland.
To be idolized—to be loved—by millions around the world.

These seem completely unreasonable dreams.
But for a boy from Gary, Indiana, who was special from the first,
they became much more than dreams.
They became fundamental needs. And they were achieved
during a lifetime that was stunning in its heights and depths,
and that was, ultimately, far, far too short.

Far too short and, sadder still,
perhaps poised for a triumphant next chapter.
We will never know.

This is the Jackson 5 version of a Pete Best photo: the lads you recognize with a drummer you don't. Michael is at the far right.
The boy behind the drum kit is Johnny Jackson, who is no relation to the brothers. He will remain anonymous, even as he continues to lay down a beat
for the boys not only in their hometown of Gary but also well into their Motown years. He was stabbed to death in Gary in 2006.

MICHAEL JACKSON'S MOTHER FELT CERTAIN early on that her fifth son was a boy apart, and maybe someone extraordinary. Having given birth to Michael on August 29, 1958, Katherine Jackson watched him develop and once said, "I don't believe in reincarnation, but you know how babies move uncoordinated? He never moved that way. When he danced, it was like he was an older person." He wasn't even singing yet.

Michael's life would be filled with oddness and paradox, and one of its central motifs is that he was perceived as older when young and younger when older. As to his precociousness, there is his mother's testimony, and there were other, similar observations. Michael's brother Jackie, one of the original Jackson 5, once told *Rolling Stone* magazine, "He was so energetic that at five years old he was like a leader. We saw that. So we said, 'Hey, Michael, you be the lead guy.' The audience ate it up." After the brothers' act was signed by Motown Records, the legendary singer and songwriter Smokey Robinson met the Jacksons and observed in Michael "a strange and lovely child, an old soul in the body of a boy."

But years later, having been deprived by the band's success of anything resembling a normal childhood, Michael found himself trying to make up for, maybe to retrieve, some of what he had missed. "I never had the chance to do the fun things kids do," he revealed. "There was no Christmas, no holiday celebrating. So now you try to compensate for some of that loss."

Thus he famously retreated into Neverland, where he became a self-styled Peter Pan—the boy who never grew up.

LONG BEFORE THAT POINT, HE WAS MICHAEL, THE cherub-cheeked front man—front boy, front kid, front tyke—of one of the most instantly beloved acts in the history of entertainment. It was all smiles when the Jackson 5, then known as the Jackson Brothers, having emerged as a local rhythm-and-blues group in Gary, lit it up at Harlem's famed Apollo Theater in 1968. The singer Gladys Knight was there that night and let Motown founder Berry Gordy know about the boys. Not long thereafter, Diana Ross was on a "Soul Weekend" bill in Gary that also featured the Jackson 5. She, too, raved about the group to Gordy, and he signed them. Their first album, released near the end of 1969, was *Diana Ross Presents the Jackson 5,* and the first hit from it, "I Want You Back," went straight to No. 1—as did "ABC," "The Love You Save," "I'll Be There" . . .

The lead voice popping out of car radios was the happy falsetto tenor of 11-year-old Michael—pitch-perfect and infectious beyond compare. He was a national celebrity overnight; even casual fans who had no idea that there was a Tito or a Jermaine in the band knew about the sensational "little Michael" up front, the kid with the oversize Afro who could sing, dance, smile and generate joy like no one else on the pop scene. The Jackson 5 grew so big, so fast that they, like the Beatles before them or the Miley Cyruses and Jonas Brothers of today, became their own cottage industry. There were T-shirts and lunch boxes, even an animated Saturday morning TV show.

As is too often the case with showbiz success stories, the behind-the-scenes experience of the Jackson 5 in no way resembled the spirited onstage performance. Only a few years earlier, another major pop group, the Beach Boys, had succeeded wildly after having been conceived as an act by the Wilson brothers' domineering, controlling father, Murry. That script was being followed closely here, but this time the situation was even worse. Joe Jackson, a crane operator for a steel company who played guitar, not only grilled and drilled his sons but routinely belittled them and would sometimes resort to physical violence. In an uncharacteristically candid 2003 interview with the British journalist Martin Bashir, Michael put it succinctly: "We were terrified of him."

An entertainment enterprise now, the Jacksons moved from their squat clapboard house in industrial Gary to an elegant home in the Los Angeles suburb of Encino. As the boys grew older, some of them went to live on their own, but Michael felt he needed the shelter of the family unit. It became increasingly clear during his teenage years—to Michael himself as well as to those who knew him well— that he had missed out on something important during his extremely atypical adolescence. Robert Hilburn, the longtime pop music critic for the *Los Angeles Times,* who had first met Michael in L.A. during the early days of the Jackson 5, recalled in a reminiscence published after the singer's death that he had once asked Michael, then in his early 20s, why he didn't move out like several of his siblings had. "Oh, no," Jackson replied. "I think I'd die on my own. I'd be so lonely. Even at home, I'm lonely. I sit in my room and sometimes cry. It is so hard to make friends, and there are some things you can't talk to your parents or family about. I sometimes walk around the neighborhood at night, just hoping to find someone to talk to. But I just end up coming home."

From left, Michael, Jermaine, Tito, Jackie and Marlon in 1971 engage in a rock 'n' roll ritual: displaying exuberance for the camera in

...anner reminiscent of the *Hard Day's Night* Beatles.

B Y THE TIME JACKSON CONFIDED HIS SENSE OF isolation to Hilburn in the early 1980s, he was long removed from the cute little boy fronting a fizzy pop band from the Midwest; he was in the midst of his transformation into the world's biggest superstar. This evolution happened gradually, and then all at once.

He mounted his first solo attempt in 1971 and enjoyed some early hits—"Got to Be There," a cover version of "Rockin' Robin," and the No. 1–charting theme song from the movie *Ben*. His dual careers throughout the 1970s—as a solo act and as the lead singer of the Jacksons, which was the new name of the erstwhile Jackson 5—were certainly successful but hardly seem predictive, today, of what was to come. He was a nice little pop star with two jobs. He actually dabbled in a third career as well, appearing as the Scarecrow in the 1978 film version of the Broadway musical *The Wiz*. Taking that gig would prove fateful.

The music supervisor of *The Wiz* was Quincy Jones, the composer, arranger, conductor and producer who had already successfully collaborated with a number of pop, jazz and rhythm-and-blues performers, perhaps most prominently Frank Sinatra. The Jacksons were now with a new record company—Epic—and for his debut solo album for this label, Michael, with Jones producing, went in a new direction. *Off the Wall* came out in 1979, and its propulsive sound caught the world's ear. Pouring forth from boom boxes everywhere were Jackson's paradoxically smooth and gritty vocals, as no fewer than four songs from the album climbed into the Top 10. Five million copies of *Off the Wall* were sold in the United States and two million more abroad. It wasn't that Michael was back—he had never left—but he was bigger than ever, perhaps. Bigger even than when he had been "little Michael."

Throughout the 1970s, he had been hurt by people wanting to preserve that younger boy in amber. Many fans of the Jackson 5 had let him know, on regular occasion, that they preferred his former self. As he was an adolescent of acute, fragile sensibility, these sentiments wounded him deeply and prompted him to seek shelter at the compound in Encino. But he never wanted to retreat from the spotlight completely. He had tasted great fame, and he yearned for the adoration of the masses again. He wanted them to adore, however, the Michael Jackson who he put forth. The redefinition of his musical and even his physical persona had begun.

And then came *Thriller* and a single performance so thrilling it changed everything.

WORKING AGAIN WITH QUINCY JONES AND bolstered by the estimable contribution of English songwriter Rod Temperton, who composed the songs "Off the Wall" and "Thriller" as well as several others on these albums, Jackson crafted what remains today the best-selling collection in the history of recorded music: *Thriller* spent two years on the *Billboard* chart, seven of its nine songs reaching the Top 10 as singles. It earned an eventual eight Grammy Awards, and an estimated 100 million copies have sold worldwide so far. But sales figures or other statistical facts cannot capture the impact that *Thriller* and the new incarnation of Michael Jackson had on world culture in the last days of 1982 and throughout 1983. This is when he entered the exclusive company of Sinatra, Elvis and the Beatles: a transcendent personality or act that changes the way that we—or at least the young among us—look, act and think. To use a cliché that is nonetheless apt and true: He was a cultural phenomenon.

The record took off overnight. Of course it did; it was superb. One after another of its songs supplanted the last at the top of the charts, and in America you could not get through the day without hearing Michael Jackson sing. You couldn't walk by a bank of TVs at Sears without seeing a Michael Jackson video playing. Then, on May 16, 1983, 50 million people sat down to watch Motown's 25th anniversary special on television. At first declining an invitation to appear, Jackson agreed to perform as a personal favor to Berry Gordy. He decided he would unveil something that he'd been working on tirelessly in front of the mirror and in his kitchen. After he and his brothers ran through a medley of their hits, Michael was left alone onstage. He struck a pose, then launched into "Billie Jean," a song he had written for *Thriller* about the groupies who, in his view, had plagued him and his brothers throughout their careers. During a musical break in the song, Jackson seemed to levitate—he floated backward in a dance step that was hard to fathom. He ended *en pointe,* and the crowd went nuts. *Entertainment Weekly* editor Steve Daly wrote later of the moonwalk: "It was a moment that crossed over in a way that no live music performance ever had. There was a messianic quality to it." The next morning, at watercoolers in every American workplace, no one was talking about anything else. That same next day, Jackson received a call from Fred Astaire, long an idol of his, complimenting him on the dancing.

That night, he had worn a black sequined jacket, a silver shirt, a black fedora, black slacks, white socks and penny loafers. He was wearing as well one white glove, also studded with sequins. Thus he had a trademark.

Later than this, Jackson would proclaim himself (or perhaps it was Elizabeth Taylor who first did, at a 1989 awards show) "the King of Pop." While some fans would go along with the title, many others would consider it needless or even desperate.

But in 1983, Michael Jackson was the cultural king of the world, a title that had been held by very few singers.

He was, by accounts, deservedly proud of this.

He thought even better and larger things were to come.

ROBERT HILBURN RECALLED IN HIS RECENT reminiscence in the *L.A. Times:* "Michael told me one night that his next album would sell twice as many copies. I thought he was joking, but he was never more serious."

The follow-up to *Thriller* was indeed a fine album, but aftershocks do not equal the earthquake itself. *Bad,* which was released in 1987, sold eight million copies domestically and 30 million worldwide, and spun off five *Billboard* No. 1 singles. That's a hugely successful record by any standard other than the one set by *Thriller.*

In live performances throughout the 1980s, Jackson played to sellout crowd after sellout crowd. Joining his brothers for their Victory Tour in 1984, which would be the Jacksons' last, Michael appeared before two million fans during 55 shows in arenas across the United States and Canada. With a total gate of $75 million, it was the largest tour ever at that time. Michael gave his $5 million in earnings to charity. His own tour in support of *Bad,* his first ever as a solo act, which ran for 16 months from 1987 to '89, set new records: 4.4 million fans at 123 concerts in 15 countries, with $125 million in ticket sales. Jackson again donated a substantial portion of his profits to charities and made sure to reserve 400 seats for underprivileged children at each of the 54 U.S. shows. Certainly the most famous of his many philanthropic efforts came in 1985 when he and Lionel Richie co-wrote "We Are the World" and, along with producer Quincy Jones, recruited a supergroup of about 40 musicians to perform it. The resulting record sold nearly 20 million copies, making it one of the best-selling singles of all time and raising millions of dollars for famine relief.

Many of Jackson's outreach efforts through the years were aimed at helping the young, and much has been written about his complicated relationship with the whole idea of childhood—a thing that, as was noted earlier, was denied him when he was himself a boy. In 1988, he bought a $17 million, 2,700-acre ranch in Los Olivos,

Michael is, in 1975, poised between being a front man in the Jackson 5 and trying to fly solo as he enjoys a sunny day in a park in Beverly Hills.

It is 1984, and the Jacksons are at the height of their powers—and Michael is flying high—as is made eminently clear at a concert in Jacksonv

▸rida, during the record-shattering Victory Tour.

California, near Santa Barbara, and turned it into not only a personal refuge but any child's idea of paradise. Spending a reported $35 million, he installed a zoo, a movie theater and an amusement park with a Ferris wheel, bumper cars, a kiddie roller coaster and half a dozen other attractions. He named his estate Neverland after the mythical world where Peter Pan, the fairy Tinker Bell and the orphaned Lost Boys dwelled.

It was in the 1980s, this period of such enormous success (in 1989 alone, he earned an estimated $125 million from album sales, endorsements and concerts), that some of Jackson's friends began expressing concern for his well-being. In trying to achieve "a dancer's body," the entertainer, who said he ate a strict vegetarian diet, clearly went through periods of dramatic weight loss. There were times when he felt faint, and some observers wondered if he was suffering from anorexia nervosa. His profile changed and so did his skin tone; Jackson later would say that he suffered from vitiligo, a pigmentation disorder, and that, counter to rumors, he was not bleaching his skin.

These various situations had not yet begun to take a toll on Jackson's immense popularity. In March 1991, Sony awarded him the largest recording contract in history, a $65 million deal, and it looked like a sound investment when that year's release, *Dangerous,* shot to No. 1 and started throwing off a fresh spate of hit singles such as "Black or White," "Remember the Time" and "Heal the World." Jackson showed a willingness on *Dangerous* to let his music evolve from the Quincy Jones sound, dabbling in the new-jack-swing style that mixed the sampling and production techniques common in hip-hop with rhythm-and-blues vocals. With seven million copies sold in the U.S. and 32 million worldwide, *Dangerous* remains the most successful new-jack-swing album ever—even if it confirmed at the time that there would never be another *Thriller.*

The Dangerous World Tour in 1992 and '93 was another triumph—3.5 million people at 67 concerts—and every dollar of Jackson's personal profit went to his new Heal the World Foundation, a relief effort that gave millions to help children endangered by war and disease. This charity also brought underprivileged kids to Neverland to ride on the rides.

When Jackson performed four songs during an electrifying Super Bowl XXVII halftime show in early 1993, it marked the first time ever that the television audience for the game actually grew during the entertainment portion, with 135 million Americans tuning in. They cheered as one when Jackson, in a gold-and-black military-style outfit, tore through "Jam," "Billie Jean," "Black or White" and "Heal the World."

There would be other triumphs for Michael Jackson, many other sellouts, much more thunderous applause. But that performance on January 31, 1993, marked perhaps the last time the reaction to him was purely rapturous and entirely unequivocal.

IN AN EFFORT TO DISPEL SOME OF THE MORE OUT-landish rumors that had been circulating about him—that he had bought the bones of the Elephant Man, that he slept in a hyperbaric oxygen chamber in hopes of achieving a kind of immortality—he began to talk about himself, but that only gave the rumors greater currency. And then others started talking about him . . . and making allegations.

Ten days after his Super Bowl appearance, Jackson sat for his first extended interview in 14 years: a 90-minute live, unedited discussion with Oprah Winfrey that was aired from Neverland. As with everything having to do with Jackson, the numbers were ridiculous: 90 million Americans watched, making it the fourth-most-viewed nonsport program in history. *Dangerous* shot back up into the Top 10 after the Winfrey show was broadcast, but Jackson, who talked movingly about his abusive father, his chronic loneliness, his skin color and other very personal matters, did little to allay the growing impression that his was a strange, damaged life. He might well have garnered sympathy, but he also created additional unease. When Jackson concluded the interview by saying, "I love what I do and I would love people to love what I do and to be loved. I just simply want to be loved wherever I go," it sounded like a plea more than a wish.

Winfrey did not talk with Jackson about his relationships with children, but this became news soon enough. The case that surfaced in the 1990s involved allegations of sexual abuse from the 13-year-old son of a friend. As an investigation began, Jackson dealt with his anxiety by taking painkillers, and he became addicted. He was supported in this period by Lisa Marie Presley, daughter of Elvis, whom he had met nearly two decades before and had now become reacquainted with. She bolstered him

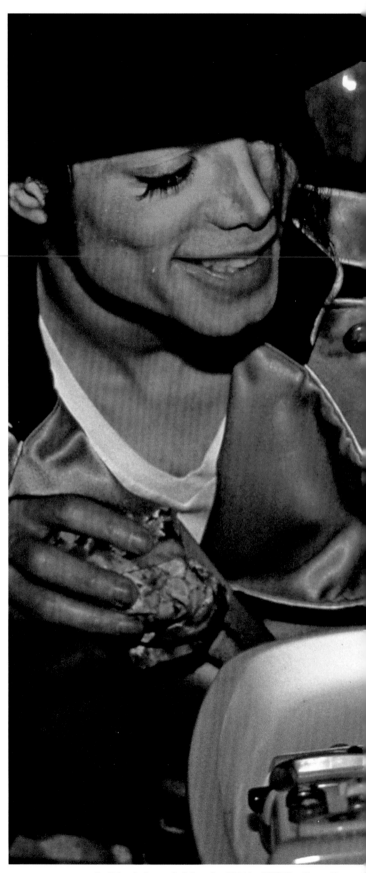

In this photograph taken for LIFE in 1997 by Harry Benson

rare photographer to be welcomed into Neverland's ultra-private inner sanctum—Jackson feeds his son, the first of two to be called Prince.

during long-distance phone conversations and tried to help as she could: "I believed he didn't do anything wrong and that he was wrongly accused, and, yes, I started falling for him. I wanted to save him. I felt that I could do it." She told Jackson to settle the allegations out of court and get himself help. He took the advice, ended the court case and reported to rehab. Then, in a later 1993 phone call, he said to Lisa Marie, "If I asked you to marry me, would you do it?" They wed quietly in the Dominican Republic, but when they were finally revealed as a married couple, the media went wild with the story— and with sniggering skepticism.

This attitude was renewed upon Jackson's death, when many of the obituaries and side stories, particularly in the tabloids, were overfilled with innuendo and unsubstantiated gossip. It is telling that Lisa Marie, who divorced Jackson within two years but stayed close to him thereafter, felt compelled to step forward and respond. "Our relationship was not a 'sham' as is being reported in the press," the now-41-year-old woman wrote on her MySpace page. "I do believe he loved me as much as he could love anyone and I loved him very much . . . I became very ill and emotionally/spiritually exhausted in my quest to save him from certain self-destructive behavior and from the awful vampires and leeches he would always manage to magnetize around him."

She wrote, "As I sit here overwhelmed with sadness, reflection and confusion at what was my biggest failure to date, watching on the news almost play by play the exact scenario I saw happen on August 16, 1977, happening again right now with Michael (a sight I never wanted to see again), just as he predicted, I am truly, truly gutted."

August 16, 1977, was the date her father, the King of Rock 'n' Roll, died at age 42 after years of substance abuse. The phrase "just as he predicted" was explained elsewhere in her posting. She recalled having a conversation about her father's death with Jackson. "At some point he paused," she wrote. "He stared at me very intensely and he stated with an almost calm certainty, 'I am afraid I am going to end up like him, the way he did.'"

THIS PRESCIENCE IS CERTAINLY, IN RETROSPECT, extremely disturbing. Here was a man in trouble, and he knew it. Realizing that he possessed this self-knowledge is beyond poignant—it is profoundly sad. And yet Jackson continued to proceed along the road of extremes and stresses, highs and lows that could not possibly lead to any kind of satisfactory equilibrium. He shattered more records with his *HIStory* double disc and world tour, drawing 4.5 million fans in 35 countries in 1996 and

'97. Meantime, upkeep of Neverland was draining him of $5 million each year, and personal expenses, including extravagant shopping sprees, were costing him half again as much. He married a second time, in 1996, to Debbie Rowe, a nurse whom he had, as with Lisa Marie, known for more than a decade (she had spent several years treating his vitiligo). They would have two children, a son and a daughter (although whether they are in fact the biological parents has been debated), and would divorce in 1999. He continued to do mammoth charity events—for Kosovo, for Guatemala, for Nelson Mandela's Children's Fund, for the Red Cross and UNESCO. He continued to make music, which sold in lesser quantities than before, and he feuded with his record company over a perceived lack of promotion. He became the father of a third child, another boy, who was birthed by a surrogate mother. He endured a second very public child abuse case, which resulted in a jury decision in 2005 that acquitted him on all counts. He left Neverland and went to live on the Persian Gulf island of Bahrain. He remained reliant on drugs, especially antidepressants.

He told the Associated Press in 2007 that if he had it to do over again, he would do the same: "I've been in the entertainment industry since I was six years old. As Charles Dickens says, 'It's been the best of times, the worst of times.' But I would not change my career . . . While some have made deliberate attempts to hurt me, I take it in stride because I have a loving family, a strong faith and wonderful friends and fans who have, and continue to, support me."

He was not wrong. At the time of his untimely death, on June 25, 2009, Michael Jackson was back in Los Angeles training and practicing for a series of comeback concerts at an arena in London. The long residency was set to begin on July 13 and last until March 6, 2010. More than a million people were hungry to see him—all 50 shows sold out immediately.

The people Michael Jackson sang to and danced for since he was a little boy still loved him deeply. They had come out for him time and time again and were anxious to come out for him once more. They would be deprived of that chance by fate, but their love would continue. When they heard the tragic news, they took to the streets and the parks and the plazas. They sang the words and tried to emulate the steps.

All of them got the lyrics and the moves perfect, but of course none of them got the entirety right. There was only one Michael Jackson, only one who could do what he could do.

There will never be another.

The Child With a Gift

I will allway love you
The Jackson Five

CBS PHOTO ARCHIVE/GETTY

MICHAEL WAS ALWAYS AT EASE IN FRONT OF A CAMERA, AS IS evident in the lovely portrait on pages 22 and 23, which was taken in Los Angeles in 1971; in the publicity photo of the Jackson 5, opposite, circa 1968; and, above, on the big stage of *The Ed Sullivan Show* in New York City on December 14, 1969. This is the first of several appearances the brothers would make on the variety program, on which Elvis and the Beatles had made history. As the host shakes Michael's hand, he congratulates the boys, whose first single, "I Want You Back," has just knocked B.J. Thomas's "Raindrops Keep Fallin' on My Head" from *Billboard*'s No. 1 spot. Michael's considerable television history will include, in 1971, not only a Jackson 5 TV special (seen on the pages immediately following) but the debut of a Saturday morning cartoon series; in 1976, a 30-minute summer variety show, *The Jacksons,* which was the first network series to star an African American family; in 1983, the legendary moonwalk on the *Motown 25* special, as well as the premiere of the 13-minute, $500,000 music video for "Thriller"; in 1993, the sensational Super Bowl performance; also in 1993, the revelatory Oprah Winfrey interview at Neverland; in 1995, a sit-down with his wife, Lisa Marie Presley, on *Primetime Live* with Diane Sawyer, which was watched by 60 million people; and many, many more appearances on myriad awards shows.

25

Michael lived until age 11 at the modest home in Gary (above), which today bears the address 2300 Jackson Street. Motown Records relocated the family to a modern house in Encino, right, in 1969. There, in 1970, LIFE photographer John Olson visited during his 15-month worldwide tour making portraits of rock stars and their parents. He fashioned pictures of Grace Slick, Joe Cocker and Ginger Baker posing lovingly with their mothers and the parents of Frank Zappa beaming proudly upon their wild and crazy son. Olson, who was by then renowned for his photography of the Vietnam War, had earlier experience "dealing with rock stars' egos and unprofessionalism, but without exception, the performers behaved like regular human beings as soon as their parents were around. They were polite, on time and not stoned." Of course that would be the case with the Jacksons whenever in the presence of the family's intimidating patriarch, Joe (rear, with his left arm on the shoulder of his wife, Katherine). It is interesting to note that this picture has never before been published; when LIFE's editors made their choices for the feature that ran in 1971, they selected a shot of just the five boys and their parents posing by the pool. They were the only Jacksons anyone cared about back then, but today it's fun to see little Janet, age four, sharing brother Jermaine's minibike. In Encino, the Jackson boys thoroughly enjoyed such hot new toys as these bikes, and all else about Southern California. Photographer Larry Schiller still remembers today his session with the group at Malibu's Paradise Cove in the late summer of 1969 (seen on the pages immediately following): "They piled in the back of my Mercedes and off we went to the beach. It was the first time they'd ever been to the ocean. As they romped along the shore, Jermaine asked, 'How cold do you think it is?' One of the other boys said he didn't know: 'I've never been in ocean water!'" Just for the record, Michael is in the yellow checkered shirt and on the yellow minibike here, and at the far right as the brothers prance about at Paradise Cove.

CIRCA 1969, MICHAEL SITS AT ATTENTION (OPPOSITE) AS MOTOWN queen Diana Ross gives her protégés, the Jackson 5, some pointers. Fifteen years older than Michael, she continued her mentoring role in his life for years and performed alongside him on stage, on television and in the 1978 film version of *The Wiz,* in which she played a rather older Dorothy and he was the Scarecrow. She said upon hearing of his death, "I am unable to imagine this. I can't stop crying. This is all too sudden and shocking." Above: In 1972, the extended Jackson brood, including Michael (second from right) and sister Janet (bottom), perform a sketch on *The Sonny & Cher Comedy Hour* (with their hostess sporting the most hair of all in the center). An interesting footnote that illustrates how bizarre the times were: The Jacksons were followed on the program by California governor and future U.S. President Ronald Reagan, cracking wise. After Michael died, Cher told CNN host Larry King that she remembered him as an "optimistic . . . beautiful . . . adorable . . . soft-spoken" boy. "God gives you certain gifts," she continued. "This child was an extraordinary child." And yet, she summed up, "He was just a kid." This must always be remembered: He was just a kid. For all the time he spent in the spotlight and in front of the camera, his smile seemed broadest and most heartfelt when playing or just hanging around—preferably with his father absent—in the backyard of the house in Encino, as we see on the pages immediately following.

MICHAEL TRIED WHEN HE COULD TO LEAD A NORMAL EXIStence—to bike around the neighborhood, to shoot hoops in the driveway, to just chill in the rec room—but it was a complicated effort. His mother was a devout Jehovah's Witness and raised her children in that faith; Michael loved her deeply and in his will asked that she be given custody of his children. His father was a holy terror, and it is illustrative of Michael's feelings toward him that he was left out of the will altogether. Joe Jackson would have belt in hand as the Jackson 5 rehearsed their routines, and if they screwed up, they felt the lash. In 1993, Michael told Oprah that at times he became physically ill upon seeing his father enter the room.

R EFUGES FOR YOUNG MICHAEL INCLUDED THE STAGE, THE studio (seen on the pages immediately following) and his driveway basketball court. This sequence of photographs taken circa 1973 is fun in and of itself, but it is interesting to note that young Michael would in fact grow to have an impact on the hoops world: just one more example of how his influence transcended music to affect many facets of our culture. In the 1980s, the rhythms and dance routines from Jackson's monster album *Thriller* were halftime staples at arenas across the land—indeed, around the world. Still today, "Billie Jean" and "Beat It" throb behind countless cheerleader routines. Jackson himself took to the court of a gritty, inner-city gym to make the music video for the explosive "Jam" from his 1991 album, *Dangerous.* His costar in that characteristically terrific production was another superstar known as MJ, the NBA legend Michael Jordan. During the course of a one-on-one session, each man busted some amazing moves. Note: If you watch the video today on YouTube, and we highly recommend that you do, stick with it for the full eight minutes. After the song ends, Jackson gives Jordan a tutorial on how to moonwalk, and it's hilarious. A postscript to the video is that Jordan's Chicago Bulls subsequently used "Jam" in a film recounting their 1992 championship season.

NEAL PRESTON

THE PHOTOGRAPHER JIM BRITT WAS WORKING FOR MOTOWN Records in the 1970s when he came to know Michael during photo shoots for the first solo albums. He remembers today the ease of a session in a Beverly Hills park that produced, in 1973, these charming, never-before-published pictures. "Things were pretty simple in those days," says Britt. "It was just Michael and me and the driver. No hair-and-makeup styl- ists, no police. It was another time and another place, for sure. I let Michael pick his clothes; I always let each guy do his own style." Michael was happy that day to show off his martial arts moves, which would, several years on, famously crop up as ele- ments in his choreography. "I never asked Michael to pose," says Britt. "I just simply encouraged my subjects to do what- ever interested them."

THE INTERNATIONAL OUTPOURING OF GRIEF THAT greeted the news of Michael Jackson's death was every bit as immense as that issuing forth in the United States. Perhaps it was even larger, for he truly was—like Muhammad Ali and precious few others—a global superstar. Some in America were, in fact, surprised to learn, in the aftermath of Jackson's death, that he had sold out those 50 upcoming arena concerts in London; they thought his luster had dimmed to the point at which such a thing was impossible. But the English fell early for Michael and remained devoted. In 1977, he and his brothers crossed the pond to perform a sold-out show at the legendary Hammersmith Odeon (below). This was well before the day when Michael would have to sequester himself during such an engagement, and so the Jacksons were free to roam London's streets and pose for the usual snaps at the usual sites—Buckingham Palace (opposite, top) and the Prime Minister's residence at 10 Downing Street, among them. When in London, this is what a tourist does. When in Switzerland, he takes to the mountains—as does Michael on the pages immediately following during a break in a 1979 European tour.

A	S WE CLOSE THIS CHAPTER OF MICHAEL'S LIFE AND HE SETS OFF to become the superstar, it is good to take a last look at the child with the gift—and at his younger sister, who would also conquer the world. Although certain of Michael's brothers would enjoy some solo success in the entertainment industry, it was Janet who, quite like Michael, would become celebrated on an almost unimaginable scale. Here, she poses with her brother at home on December 18, 1972, completely unaware of what the future has in store. Shortly after his death, she appeared onstage at the BET Awards in Los Angeles and, speaking before a projection of this very photograph, said, "My entire family wanted to be here tonight, but it was too painful. To you, Michael is an icon. To us, Michael is family. And he will forever live in all of our hearts." She added, "On behalf of my family and myself, thank you for all of your love, thank you for all of your support. We miss him so much."

A Thriller Like No Other

ON THE PAGES IMMEDIATELY PREVIOUS, MICHAEL JACKSON performs in L.A. at the 1995 MTV Video Music Awards alongside Slash, the Guns N' Roses guitarist, who played on Jackson's *Dangerous* and *HIStory*. In this period, Jackson is the biggest entertainer in the world. A crucial association that would help him reach that status was made during work on the film version of the musical *The Wiz* (Jackson is the Scarecrow, above). The music supervisor on that movie was Quincy Jones (right, with Jackson at the United Negro College Fund Awards in New York City in 1988). Jones would help Jackson craft *Off the Wall* (1979) and *Thriller* (1982), both of which would send him to the top. Opposite: In 1983, Jackson and his brother Jermaine rehearse for their appearance at the Motown 25 celebration, which will subsequently air as a TV special. When America sees Michael moonwalk during his solo spot on that show, the entertainer's fame climbs ever higher. By the time the Jacksons launch their Victory Tour the following year, Michael is far and away the hottest draw in showbiz. LIFE magazine sent its technological wizard of a photographer, Henry Groskinsky, to capture the grandiosity of that tour when it encamped at the Gator Bowl in Jacksonville, Florida. Groskinsky executed the assignment splendidly, as the results on the following pages testify.

I N A 1984 PHOTOGRAPH FOR *LIFE* TAKEN BY THE NOTED portraitist Lynn Goldsmith and at a 1985 appearance in London, Jackson is magisterial. The mob scene, which rivals those that once attended the Beatles, is for a relatively trivial matter—Jackson is about to attend the unveiling of his likeness at the Madame Tussaud's Wax Museum—and attests to the magnitude of the singer's recent leap in celebrity status. Jackson's 1980s were the equivalent of the Fab Four's 1960s and Elvis's 1950s. He defined the decade.

ONLY THE MOST PRESTIGIOUS OF CITIZENS ARE GIVEN A private tour of the Oval Office by the President of the United States, as Jackson, appropriately dressed for the occasion, is by Ronald Reagan in May 1984 (above). At the time, Jackson is doing his part to publicize the President's campaign against drunk driving. Opposite: Only the most prestigious of singers are invited to provide the halftime entertainment at the Super Bowl, as Jackson is in 1993. Here, he leaps in a blaze of glory during an incendiary performance that actually boosts the television audience for the game—an unprecedented feat. In the week after his appearance in Pasadena, Jackson's album *Dangerous* soars 90 places on the *Billboard* chart. He will have little time to savor this triumph, as the first public allegations of child abuse are looming on the horizon, as is an addiction to prescription drugs that will continue to plague him for the rest of his days.

THROUGHOUT HIS LIFE, THE OFTEN LONELY AND TRAGICALLY insecure Jackson leaned, when he could, on family and friends. On these two pages, he is seen at a gathering of Clan Jackson at the family place in Encino. Despite the traumas suffered in his youth, he and his father never severed ties, and he was happy to visit at Joe and Katherine's home. He would talk regularly on the phone with his siblings and remained close to his brothers, although after the Victory Tour he resisted occasional entreaties to take the Jacksons act back on the road. The so-called First Family of Soul had its occasional rough patches, but stayed a tight unit.

HERE WE SEE FOUR WOMEN WITH WHOM HE HAD CLOSE RELATIONSHIPS. Opposite, top left, is Tatum O'Neal (in 1979), and at right is Brooke Shields (in 1984). Elizabeth Taylor (in 1985) is at the bottom, and above, Michael strolls in Neverland with his wife, Lisa Marie Presley. It is at least interesting and perhaps fascinating that these women were all, like Jackson, in the public glare while young—three were child stars and the fourth was the daughter of the ultra-famous Elvis. They could understand one another: the aspirations, the pressures. Presley's support during Jackson's crises in 1993 led to love, but she felt she had to leave when it became clear that she could not help him.

HARRY BENSON

FIRST IN 1993 AND THEN AGAIN IN 1997, JACKSON INVITED LIFE and the photographer Harry Benson to enter the gates of Neverland. As we wrote in the '93 feature, "Until now, Neverland has never been seen in such detail by outsiders, except for busloads of children, many terminally ill, whom Jackson invites for field trips." Sixteen years later, that assertion remains true—there is no photography from inside Neverland remotely this intimate—and with Jackson's death, we felt these pictures should come back home. And so a selection is presented here in this LIFE commemorative.

On the two pages immediately previous, Jackson plays Pied Piper in 1993 for the children of some of Neverland's 70 full-time employees. On these pages, that tour of the grounds continues, with Jackson front and center on the Ferris wheel (above), riding shotgun in a bumper car (opposite, top right) and pointing out Tinker Bell in the dominant piece in his art collection, a painting by David Nordahl that looms over the foyer. Two stories tall, the canvas is one of six tableaux in the mansion showing Michael amidst a sea of children.

67

THE DECEMBER 1997 *LIFE* STORY FROM NEVERLAND WAS entitled "The King as 'Pop,'" and it was largely a celebration of Michael's first child, then-nine-month-old "Prince" Michael Joseph Jackson Jr. The caption for the photograph opposite read: "Perched on a throne in Dad's bedroom, father and son get the royal treatment, thanks to two baby nurses (pacifiers at the ready) on call around the clock." The photograph above appeared on the magazine's cover. In that period, Jackson and his son were sharing meals, afternoon naps and story hour. "I put my voice on tape, reading poems, stories I've written," Jackson told LIFE. "When I'm out at concerts, [his nurses] play it for him." Prince's mother, Debbie Rowe, was said to be rarely around and was altogether absent during LIFE's visit. In the nursery, the nannies came and went, bottles and squeeze toys in tow. Six teddies occupied an antique African cradle, six stuffed animals crowded Prince's crib. Above it hung a Humpty Dumpty poster, a Mickey and Minnie mobile and a quilt with Daddy's image. "You don't have to buy him much," said Jackson. "Fans give him toys, signs, banners—everything."

W HEN *LIFE* VISITED NEVERLAND IN 1997, JACKSON SAID
he had undergone a recent burst of inspiration thanks
to his son: "I've written more songs in my life—
albums' worth—because of him than because of any
other inspiration. He's complete inspiration." A sam-
ple lyric: "People say / I'm not O.K. / 'cause I love such
elementary things. / It's been my fate / to compensate /
for the childhood I've never known." Just so, and a
lifelong occupation for Michael Jackson. Here we see
him escaping with ways he knows best: into music and
in a contemplative session on Neverland's swing set.

D EBBIE ROWE AND JACKSON WERE WED ON NOVEMBER 14, 1996 (above), and divorced after three years of marriage. They became the parents of two children, who remained in Jackson's care after the split. Michael would become the father of one more son, this one *formally* named Prince—Prince Michael Jackson II—and at right we have a procession from the Beverly Hills Hotel on May 16, 2009, that includes siblings Michael Joseph Jackson Jr. and Paris Michael Katherine Jackson and then Prince II. Trailing, but not wearing one of the masks he insists his children don in public, is Jackson— who at this point has barely a month to live. The poignancy of this picture is palpable, as is that of the one on the pages immediately following, which was taken in New York City during the HIStory Tour in 1997. What was the boy thinking about the future, when he sang way back then? And what was the man thinking of the past?

73

Gone
Too Soon

IN A WORLD FUELED AND FED BY THE INTERNET, THE WORD spread instantly on June 25, 2009, and the tributes and celebrations and vigils and wakes blossomed nearly as fast. On the preceding pages, the Apollo Theater in Harlem, New York, where the Jackson 5 won an amateur night contest in 1967, became a gathering place. As did (counterclockwise from opposite, top) Hitsville, the Motown Records Museum in Detroit; the borders of the Jackson family property in Encino, California; Trafalgar Square in London; a prison yard in the Philippines, where 1,500 incarcerated men reprised a version of the "Thriller" dance they had made famous on YouTube years before; and Paris, under the Eiffel Tower. Many mourned, many sang, many cried, many sighed. All agreed that it was very, very sad that Michael Jackson had left us—so early, so soon.

FAREWELL

Michael Jackson
1958–2009